D1616425

Honoring

Your Child's Spirit

Honoring
Your Child's Spirit

*Pre-Birth Bonding and
Communication*

Flo Aeveia Magdalena

**Illustrations & Editing
Jayn Stewart**

For information contact:
All Worlds Publishing
P.O. Box 603
Plantsville, CT 06479
Tel. (866) 235-1350
Fax (860) 276-9539

Published by: All Worlds Publishing

First Edition 2008. Trade Paper.
Printed in USA

Includes bibliographical references

ISBN 978-1-880914-10-6

For information on more ways to
support your journey,
contact
Soul Support Systems
18 The Square, Suite 20 • Bellows Falls, VT 05101
(802) 463-2200
www.SoulSupportSystems.org
SoulSupportSystems@verizon.net

My Gratitude to....

Jayn Stewart for her expertise in editing and illustrating this book, which has taken 16 years to birth. Her continued presence in the unfolding of this process for supporting mothers and babies has been invaluable to the evolution and manifestation of this book. I deeply appreciate her dedication and awareness of the importance of this work.

Christy Adams for her diligence, patience, and expertise in creating the formatting for this book, grounding and guiding my ideas, and assisting me to language my creation.

Maggie Scobie, who first asked me to bring forth guidance to pregnant and new mothers at the Light Center in Washington, DC in 1991.

Cathrine Estar for her generosity and support in providing her home in Tucson as we finalized the book.

Teresa Robertson for her guidance, information, and experience.

Karuna Kress for editing assistance and support.

Those who were drawn to be present for the initial sharing of information from the spiritual realms and guidance from The Ones With No Names about how to raise children in light.

All of you who give continued support to this work and to the fulfillment of a million years of dreaming— the choice for peace on Earth.

**Previously Released Books
by
Flo Aeveia Magdalena**

I Remember Union: The Story of Mary Magdalena

Sunlight On Water: A Manual for Soul-full Living

Contents

Foreword

As far back as I can remember, I have questioned why it is so challenging for human beings to live in harmony with each other. I am hopeful that as our species learns, grows, and evolves—at times reaching back to incorporate the teachings of ancient cultures and wisdom traditions—new pathways will open to us, showing us how to lessen competition, encourage individual expression, and support all life.

My search to discover tools that will assist us in co-creating from the heart began with religion and science, and included both rational and intuitive models. An understanding of the "new" science, which is based on the interrelationship among all things, provided me with answers to these long-standing questions. Just knowing that we are all interconnected, and therefore cannot be separated, leads me to ask, *How can we utilize this connection in all our relationships to create a deeper harmony and union?*

In this book, I share some of the ways I have found to feel connected with others and to bring the promise of harmony among humanity to fruition. In my vision of this promise, we will become kinder, dearer, and more wise. We will raise our children with deep honor and respect for themselves, for each other, and for the earth. The gap of feeling separate will close, and we will be a single generation of different ages living from the heart as one.

~ ~ ~ ~ ~ ~ ~ ~ ~

I once had an uplifting and life-changing conversation with an African man who shared his tribe's traditions on birthing. He told me that the tribe's shaman, or medicine man, would connect with the soul of each child before birth. The shaman would arouse the pregnant woman in the middle of the night, take her outside under the starlit sky, and speak to the child's soul. In this way, he came to know the child and what it wanted to learn and contribute in its lifetime. Once the shaman understood the child's purpose, he would share this information with the tribe. The whole tribe would prepare to receive the newborn, deciding what training, trade, or skill would best fulfill the child's purpose and identifying those who would best support the child's growth.

In other African tribes, the shaman connects with the soul of the unborn by hearing its "heart song." Before the child is born, the shaman sings the child's song to the expectant mother and other tribal members. During the child's birth, the whole tribe sings the song and welcomes the new one to life. The song of each person is unique and is sung at initiation, marriage, during significant times such as challenge or danger, and at the time of passing again into the spirit world. Even more importantly, if a member violates a law or tradition, he or she is called into the center of a community circle. The tribe sings that member's heart song, knowing that hearing this song will bring the person into alignment once again. The tribe recognizes that the individual's behavior is simply a result of not being connected to their spirit.

I can only imagine how it must feel to be held, heard, and sung to by your tribe or family for your entire lifetime. I deeply believe that society suffers when the bond with our spirit goes unseen, unheard, and unacknowledged, particularly by those who are close to us. This book offers simple and natural ways to acknowledge your child's spirit so that you may "hear" his or her unique heart song.

The thought of bringing forth a child and the promise of this new life is exciting! We know that each child is a special gift, and we want our sons and daughters to learn, grow, and live their fullest potential. We hope that they will bring something unique and special to the world that will make it a better place.

Becoming a parent involves significant physical, emotional, mental, and spiritual preparation. *Honoring your Child's Spirit: Pre-Birth Bonding and Communication* is the first of a four-book series that focuses primarily on the *spiritual* aspects of raising children. In this book you will learn how to connect and bond with the spirit, or essence, of your unborn child. As you establish this sensory bond with your child, you are able to really "get" who they are. You know them inside out, and they know you just as thoroughly. The initial bond becomes even deeper as you go through the birthing process and the child grows and matures.

Many parents today are creating their families somewhat differently from the way they were raised. As relationships are based more on honoring the essence of each person, no matter the age, there is less need to live from beliefs, conditioning, and assigned "roles." We see this in changing family structures where dads stay at home, focusing less on monetary responsibilities and more on creating a deep emotional bond with their children.

One mother of four said, "When I brought my second son home, I held him in my arms and rocked him. As I looked into his eyes, I knew that he did not 'belong' to me. He came through me, but he was not 'mine.' I had felt this with my other children, but somehow it came home to me with my last child. It was so clear that he was part of something much larger. This points to a greater truth for all of us—we are not who we think we are, and we do not 'belong' to the roles we assign ourselves and each other. The true nature of our children knows nothing of 'roles.' They are in a word *free.*"

Since the family system is our first and most intimate experience of the world, it is where we learn about love, sharing, generosity, honoring, and co-creation—or, on the other hand, about hate, reaction, fear, anger, and separation. Family interactions cause us to grow or shrink, to open or withdraw. The family may be a spiritual haven and a loving place of growth or a place of absent presence, where we physically live together but do not connect. We either make this connection and create a foundation in our childhood or spend the rest of our lives looking for it.

Honoring Your Child's Spirit: Pre-Birth Bonding and Communication illustrates how the heart/soul connection works in families. When both the mother and the father establish a conscious heart/soul connection with their children and with each other, deeper levels of trust and safety are experienced.

As we deepen our bonds, we become more aware of each other. We are more sensitive to the subtle, nonverbal communication which we exchange at all times (whether we know it or not) with all living organisms. Science tells us that there is an energetic field which radiates around our body. Even though we can't see it, necessarily, this field can be felt, and we know it is there. We experience this field, for example, in response to what we sense in a room that we have just entered where others are present. We might feel harmony and peacefulness, or discord and anger.

In each family or relationship grouping, as the individual

fields interact, a larger shared field is created. Realizing that this occurs helps us understand our responses to others and why we may feel connected to or disconnected from them. Hereditary patterns, ancestral events, traumatic life experiences, educational and religious dogmas and family beliefs have all shaped how we relate consciously and unconsciously in a "field" sense. Sometimes we are afraid to move too close to someone. Sometimes we are uneasy in certain situations or with certain individuals, but we don't know why. We can be afraid to sing, create, love, speak our truth, or just be.

These fears are most often conditioned by our life experiences. They are also influenced by the conscious and unconscious patterns we have developed in our family of origin. Awareness of the subtle, invisible ways we have been connected with others can help us be more conscious about our patterns of relationship. In creating our own family, we can relate from a place of honoring and co-creation with the intention to develop a harmonious field that sustains all family members.

When a woman is pregnant, her field and her child's field are shared. The child also feels his or her own individual being. There is really no separation between them. They are just in different energetic fields. When the child is born and the two fields separate, the child experiences this separation. Ways to lessen this feeling of separation and assist the child and mother to stay connected throughout the birthing process are offered in this book.

Relating primarily from the heart and honoring each person's essence, we can live together with more wisdom, knowing, and respect and less discomfort and conflict. There is little need to compete when we live from our truth instead of from conditioned beliefs. We hear others' points of view, share ideas, and cooperate as we make our way in the world. We want everyone's voice to be heard. We become more comfortable with the heart and soul as the way we experience the world.

By honoring your spirit, the spirit of your child, and the spirit in all things, you are a vital link in an important understanding—we are all born from one light that infuses all life. A new world begins with the birth of each child. Thank you for making the contribution of your child's life. It will make all the difference!

Flo Aeveia Magdalena

Introduction

Exercises in this book are designed primarily to develop the relationship between mother and child. Since husbands and significant others, family members and friends may also be eagerly awaiting the birth, guidance is also offered for them in how to create a soul-to-soul connection.

Communicating with your child throughout your pregnancy offers many opportunities to reshape the cultural, familial, and societal constraints you are asked to live within. Identifying existing patterns and making new choices can reshape your world and the world of your unborn child. Through the instruction you offer your child and from what you learn about your own patterns and the patterns of those with whom you relate, you can develop ways to live from a place of centered, connected, and creative peace. It is as easy as sensing and acknowledging what is real for you and recognizing what has and hasn't worked. Living from your knowing, you bring forth that which resides in your heart, dispelling the lingering doubts and patterns that have shaped your world unconsciously.

We invite mothers to practice the visualizations, prayers, and exercises with clear intention. Relax, breathe deeply into your belly, and let yourself settle into the experience. Mothers who use these exercises as a special time of connection, or as a ritual, find that they create a reverent space in which to communicate with their baby. They also say that being in this deep space brings the sacredness of *all* life more fully into their everyday experience. We suggest ways to use the exercises, but know that you can create whatever ways work for you. You may find that you are more comfortable with some of the exercises than others. You are unique and what you are drawn to is perfect and beneficial for you and your baby.

Keeping a journal and/or drawing pictures of your thoughts, feelings, and experiences during your pregnancy is a good way to show how the relationship and communication are developing between you and your unborn child. When you re-read your first entries or look at the pictures you have drawn, you can see how your love has grown and your connection has been nurtured. This is one way to be more aware of the miracle that you are co-creating.

The blessings and rituals are from "The Birthing" chapter of *I Remember Union: The Story of Mary Magdalena*. It is strongly recommended that you read this chapter in its entirety to feel the flow of the rituals before using them. (This chapter is in the Appendix, page 101.)

The blessings can be given at any time during a child's life, not just at birth. In one California family, a mom uses these rituals with her three children, ages 7-13, to deepen their sense of security and belonging. The oldest child prepares for tests and sporting events, releasing anxiety and bringing in her highest potential. The middle child aligns with her inner nutritional balance and builds more self-confidence, and the youngest reduces his high energy in a positive way rather than allowing frustration to build.

Another family in South Dakota bestows the blessings to each family member in their weekly meetings. These rituals, which may include the newborn, parents, siblings, grandparents, and friends, bring the sacred light of all creation into the heart of each person. Many individuals honor their own lives by reading the blessings to themselves.

You can remake the world from your own experience and communicate that effectively to your child—without words. Claim your place, your power, and that of your unborn child. It is all about sharing your hearts with each other and creating a strong family foundation where each member experiences a world that is safe and nurturing.

Join us now as we enter the world of your unborn child...

Pre-Birth
Bonding and
Communication

Chapter One

Communicating With Your Child

Imagine that you are a pulsing spark of light, a life force held in a container, a womb, and that you relate only through your senses. You give and receive through your center—the area of your heart. The pulse of life moves through you and around you, forming an energetic field.

You know that you are connected to all aspects of life and that your spirit is part of the larger universe. Your point of connection to this universe is through your Seed of Light—the point of light that you carry like a signature just below your heart. You are an intricate and beautiful part of the unfolding universe, sensitive to the pulses that sustain you. You are nurtured and taken care of in an organic, natural way.

You also hear and feel what is happening in the environment outside your container. You sense differences in temperature. You respond to emotional changes in that environment.

Your awareness grows and expands. Every moment you are more able to sense what it will be like to be spirit in physical form, anticipating your birth, feeling the family to which you will be born, and becoming responsive to your mother and her environment. Your responses to the external world do not, at this point, have a way to be expressed unless a bridge to that world is created without language.

Chapter Two

Connecting Without Words

The possibility of connecting with your unborn child is amazing and wondrous! As soon as you know you are pregnant, you can begin a nonverbal connection that involves sending and receiving love. You can contact the spirit of your child through the bond that is already developing between you.

The following exercises help you establish an energetic connection with your baby. Use your imagination to visualize the link between you and feel your connection. You might experience this as a subtle sensation in your body or as colors around or within your energy fields. There is no right or wrong here. Just relax into these exercises and see what happens. And don't worry if nothing seems to happen right away. Just keep practicing. Once you make the intention to connect, it begins on a subtle level. Sometimes the mind is the last to know!

Touching In Without Words

1. Sit quietly.

2. Take three or four deep breaths and settle into your body.

3. Make the intention to touch into the world of your child.

4. Imagine your womb, your child's container.

5. Using your imagination, create a link with your child.

6. Foster a connection through your thoughts and feelings. There are no expectations, demands, or challenges - just an inner experience. You are building an energetic bridge between your world and your child's world.

7. Take a deep breath and let the visualization subside.

Touching In Without Words

Connecting Your Energy Fields

1. Sit quietly.

2. Take three or four deep breaths and settle into your body.

3. Make the intention to connect with your child's energy field.

4. First, make your field glow by sending your thoughts and intention to it.

5. Next, make your baby's field glow by sending your thoughts and intention to it. Imagine both fields as circles.

6. Stay with this visualization for a few minutes. What do you observe or feel?

7. Take a deep breath and let the visualization subside.

Connecting Your Energy Fields

Teresa Robertson, a midwife and birthing intuitive, has been working with pregnant mothers for over 20 years. She has found that the following exercises assist mothers in bonding and communicating with their unborn children.

The Bubble Meditation

It is important to create a method of connecting with your baby in which there are *clear energy boundaries* so you are aware of where you begin and the baby ends.

1. Sit quietly. Take a deep breath. Ground your body. To do this, feel an imaginary connection from the base of your spine, as wide as your hips, to the center of the earth. You might visualize an X at the base of your spine and an X at the center of the earth and connect them with a tree trunk, waterfall, anchor, or any other image that works for you.

2. Imagine an empty bubble outside your body. It might be in front of your face or in front of your heart. Ground this bubble to the center of the earth with its own cord. (This method works best when the woman is not yet pregnant. For pregnant women, imagine that you can see into your uterus.)

3. Invite the spirit of your unborn child to fill this bubble. To facilitate the connection, you might see a tube of light extending from you to the bubble and the baby's heart. (If you are already pregnant, you can also place your hands on your belly, like an ultra-sound transducer, to pick up information.)

4. Be aware of what you see, feel, hear, or sense about this bubble. Write down or draw your experiences.

Now that you have grounded your body and established a connection with your baby, you can begin your first conversation.

Starting A Conversation

1. At your crown chakra (located on the top of your head) visualize a gold ring. It says, "Hello, I see you." Send that gold-ring-hello to your unborn baby's bubble. Notice what your baby's reaction is to the hello. What happens to its bubble? Do the colors and/or images around your baby change? Does your body feel different?

2. Now ask your baby if he/she has anything to tell you. Be aware of your body. If it feels like nothing is happening, ask the baby's spirit to offer its information in a manner that is clear and understandable to you.

3. To close your conversation, send a golden "Good-bye" ring (in the same way you sent the hello) to the baby's bubble.

4. Take some time to journal, draw, or do some other artwork to integrate your experience. When you set the focus of communicating with your unborn child in play and joy, you receive much more information.

Enjoy the experience!

As your connection with your child deepens, invite other family members to communicate with the baby. You might want to start with the father or partner, a grandparent, or a sibling. Ask the person to sit quietly near you. Tell the individual how you visualize, or sense, your own energy field and that of your baby. You might offer suggestions as to how the other person could do this, but each one will do it in his or her own way. You might be surprised at what you hear, especially from children, who can easily "tune in" to the spirit of another. What do they see, feel, or hear? Do they sense the baby's spirit or essence?

Pre-birth connection touches not only the spirit and soul of the child, but also the spirit and soul of each family member. When you foster a spiritual connection with your children before birth, you feel your *own* spirit and life force more deeply.

Chapter Three

The Life's Blueprint

Many ancient traditions hold the belief that the soul lives many lifetimes. Each lifetime has a particular design or "blueprint" that includes what one wishes to learn and contribute to the world. Imagine that before birth each of us has a powerful and beautiful experience where we see everything—our past, present, and future. As we review our previous life experiences and learnings, we decide upon the blueprint for our next life. We choose many things—including our parents, the date, place, and time of our birth—that can best support us in living our life's design. All our earthly experiences, even the painful ones, will potentially help us learn and grow.

Some children, even at an early age, can tell you why they are here. One 10-year-old boy, who had been writing poems at school and at home for several days, said to his teacher and classmates, "I've learned something from writing these poems. In each one of them I mention peace. What I'm learning about myself is that peace is a very important part of my life. Maybe I'm here to bring peace and harmony in some way." A child may be aware that an important part of her life's design is to make music or bring joy to people through song and dance. Another may know that his special gift is his ability to communicate with animals and nature. Others are drawn to the world of science and technology. Some know that they will be teachers, business people, ministers, doctors and healers, artists, homemakers and parents—the list is endless. Many children do not yet know what their path will be, but they may be able to tell you something about their essence. For example, one girl said, "I don't know what I will do when I grow up, but I do know that I love the oceans and the sea creatures."

Toni Petrinovich, Ph.D, a spiritual counselor and teacher, says, "First and foremost, it is important that new parents realize that the *true* gift of the child is in its coming to earth at this time. Whatever the child does or becomes is an outward symbol of its earthly blueprint. The light of the child in its awareness and consciousness *is* the gift."

The more we are honored as souls, even before birth, the more likely we are to remember who we are and why we have come. When we acknowledge that we are spiritual beings in physical bodies, we also realize that we have the inherent wisdom to guide our lives. We feel deeply connected to ourselves and all life, and we can live our lives in a way that more deeply reflects our purpose.

Chapter Four

The Seed of Light

Each of us has a place in our body that houses what is called the Seed of Light. Information from our soul is available to us through the Seed, which sends out a vibrational signal about who we are and what we are here to do. Our Seed of Light holds not only our individual blueprint, but also the larger design for humanity—our potential to live in cooperation within all our diversity.

When parents align with their own Seed and connect with their child's Seed, it is easier for both parent and child to live their designs and to honor each other's strengths and differences. When we connect with our children before birth through our Seeds of Light, it helps them make the transition from spirit into form more easily. Another way to say this is that when a bridge of light is established between the child's spirit and its physical body while it is in utero, it is easier for the child to maintain that bond after birth.

Your Seed of Light, which looks like a diamond, is located in the center of your chest at the point that divides the left and right rib cage. This point is called the xiphoid process.

The Seed of Light

Chapter Five

Connecting With Your Child's Seed of Light

Connecting your Seed and the Seed of your child happens naturally in the field of energy that you share during pregnancy. There is no difference in the place of the universe where the child is and the place where you are. Recognizing that there is no distance between you is the first step in creating the bridge to nonverbal communication. You can create this bridge at any time during your pregnancy.

The connection accomplishes three purposes:

- You bond with your child through a bridge of light.

- You communicate from your soul to your child's soul.

- You become aware of the energy field that you share.

Connecting With Your Child's Seed of Light

1. Sit quietly.

2. Take a few deep breaths and settle into your body.

3. Make the intention to connect with your child's Seed of Light.

4. Connect with your own Seed by placing your fingers in the center of your chest where the ribs come together in a point. Relax. Breathe. Imagine that your breath is going in and out of this point.

5. Focus on this point until you feel your Seed of Light respond. The sensation may be warmth, tingling, pulsing, or simply a sense of connection.

6. Be aware of any images, senses, awareness, memories, or possibilities that surface. This is your inner wisdom, your inner voice, your inner knowing. Enjoy this and stay with it for a while.

7. When you feel ready, create the connection to your child's Seed of Light, which is located in the center of the baby's body. Visualize this as just outside your body in a small energy field.

8. Feel this connection for a few minutes.

9. Send an arc of light from your Seed to your child's Seed. Now send a strand of golden thread to your child. Weave this thread back and forth between your Seeds, joining them together.

10. Strengthen your bond through the golden thread, weaving it back and forth. As you do this, you may feel a sensation, quickening, or warmth. You may feel the connection in your heart, your Seed of Light, or in your body.

11. There is no specific way that this has to happen. Take your time. Just enjoy the merging of your energetic fields. Get to know each other. Very gently receive impressions and begin communication.

12. When you feel complete, rest in the beautiful field that you have created together.

13. Take a deep breath and let the visualization subside. Journal about your experience.

When you first touch into the soul of another, the sensation may be subtle. Take your time. Try not to have a preconceived notion of how it will feel. Something physical may happen so that you know you are connected, but not necessarily. Instead of asking yourself, *Did I do it? What happened?* just relax and receive whatever comes.

Once you are comfortable connecting with your child's Seed, you may deepen the experience by practicing the next exercise.

Deepening the Connection

Deepening the Connection

1. Make the intention to deepen your connection with your child's Seed of Light.

2. As you bond with your child, stay with the sensation or experience for a few minutes, then increase the time that you sustain the bond.

3. Practice bonding when you first awaken, during the day, and at night to make the connection frequent and natural. Establish a daily check-in time where you share with your child how things are going during the day and what is happening for you. Begin a dialogue with questions such as *How are you? Is there anything you need?*

4. Be aware of sensations that arise during this communication.

5. Send love to your child through your Seed and sense if love is returned.

6. Now send an idea and sense whether your child has understood. Shift the focus from giving to receiving so that you feel this exchange deepen.

7. Tell your child about yourself. What do you love? What brings you joy? How have you developed your own spirit? What do you long to bring to the world?

8. Ask your child what he or she will need to assist its spiritual growth and health.

9. Take a deep breath and let the visualization subside. Write or draw your experiences in your journal.

As you deepen your communication with your child, you may want to share things that are part of your life, including diet, rest, and exercise. What is easy for you? What is difficult? What are you afraid of? What are you proud of? Ask your baby if there is anything in your diet that he or she would rather you not eat. One mother said that when she asked her unborn child this question, her daughter told her that she would like her mother to stop eating broccoli and drinking coffee. But she *did* like her to eat fruits such as pears, peaches, and bananas.

At this point you might start projecting pictures from your mind or imagination of what you look like and how you feel inside when you are sad, angry, afraid, confident, serious, silly, joyful, or playful. Laugh at yourself and show your child how your moods change. Let your baby know that moods are sometimes caused by what is happening to you in the world. These feelings are *your* responsibility, however, and your child need not feel responsible for your happiness.

Singing, humming, chanting, or toning with your child can assist in your bonding experience. Information about the importance of communicating through sound is offered by Giselle Whitwell in the Appendix.

The quality of your exchange strongly affects your relationship. You are each building a sense of the other that is visceral and tangible. As you come to know each other, soul to soul, your child will understand your moods, dreams, fears and needs. And you may understand why your child needs and wants certain things, or why he or she is afraid of something. Pre-birth communication can go a long way in minimizing misunderstandings and challenges that may arise later as your child grows.

The relationship you are developing is not bound by normal restrictions because the information that is sent via channels of sensory response is unaffected by language, beliefs, or convention. As you and your child develop this non-verbal way to communicate, your husband, partner or significant other can enter into this bond as well. Together you can establish a way to feel connected beyond earthly rules, and can therefore create a unique relationship that works for your family.

The energetic bridge you build between you and your child can also help you communicate about important decisions that need to be made. These may include such things as the birthing itself, the home environment—anything that would help your child feel more comfortable during pregnancy and after birth. Such communication can help your baby trust the birth process. It can also help you be more positive and "present" during the birth. This is important for the child because the birth experience sets the foundation for its life.

Chapter Six

Connecting With Your Child's Energy Field

Connecting with your child's energy field is another way to get to know his or her body, emotion, mind and spirit. This field is part of the larger electromagnetic field (EMF) that we all share. The EMF surrounds all living things and is how we are all interconnected. Whether we realize it or not we, as organisms, are constantly relating with each others fields.

The following diagram shows the fields of the mother and child communicating. It may be easier to imagine the child's field around you instead of within you the first few times you do this exercise. Notice that there is a large bubble or circle for the large EMF, and then each of you has your own field or bubble.

Connecting with the energy field of another person teaches us to sense our own field more distinctly in our relationships with others. As mother and baby relate through the field, there is an ever-growing comfort and ease.

Connecting With Your Child's Energy Field

1. Sit or lie quietly.

2. Take three or four deep breaths.

3. Make the intention to connect with your child's energy field.

4. Close your eyes and relax all parts of your body.

5. Imagine floating or lying on a surface that supports you. Feel your muscles relax. Let go. Continue relaxing and letting go for five or six minutes. Feel the rhythm of your breathing.

6. Imagine that your child's field is a small ball of light in front of you. Send an invitation to that light to connect with you. The essence of your child understands and will be there to share this. You are developing a new sensory experience, so give yourself time.

7. Send light out from your heart or Seed of Light and join with the ball of light of your child.

8. Imagine your light and the child's light becoming one—a flow of light coming from your heart, moving to join with your child's light, and then making the two of you one pulsating light.

9. Anchor the sensation of the two of you as one by remaining connected as long as you like.

10. Take a deep breath and let the visualization subside.

Connecting With Your Child's Energy Field

Chapter Seven

Connecting Everyone Together

Since our energy field is an important way that we connect with others, it is helpful to be aware of your field, the fields of those with whom you live, and the larger field that exists among the important people in your life. Your body has a response to each person. One way to understand this response is to create an image in your mind of the family's collective field. How does each person connect with you? How do you connect with them? How can your child relate with each person? Let your child know about the sensation that each person gives you. Share your observations about your child's father, or your partner, your child's siblings, grandparents, and others who will be significant in his or her life.

For example, this is a picture of Uncle John. (Send an image of Uncle John to your baby.) He is older and fragile, and we take care of him in our home. He will be part of your life as you grow up.

When you feel ready, invite your husband or partner, family members and friends to observe how you and your child connect your Seeds of Light. Share with them how it works and feels, and how the baby gives impressions and information to you. They can then practice connecting their Seed with that of your child. Compare notes. Is communication the same or different? This practice is valuable for the baby in particular, because it helps him sense the individual and collective energy fields he will be relating to after he is born. It helps him adjust to and prepare for his new life and physical surroundings.

The Larger Fields Where We All Co-Exist

Chapter Eight

Place Your Child In Light

There is a strong difference between the spiritual and the material worlds. Think for a moment about the distinction between spirit and form, light and density. The spiritual dimension is light, or vibration. The earth dimension is form, or matter. When the child is placed in light before and during birth, she feels a bridge of light welcoming her to the world. When that bridge is consciously created during the birth experience, birth can be easier for both mother and baby. If the experience of light is not available to the child, she can feel disoriented as the physical separation with her mother occurs.

Because the physical world is denser than the spiritual world, most children experience some amnesia at birth about their light and purpose. To make the transition from spirit to form easier, it is important to place light in the baby's body, the birth canal, the environment where she will be born, and the place where she will live. When you do this, she will be assured that you are there and that light still surrounds her, no matter where she is. She will be more comfortable in physical form. The moment of birth is a defining moment for the child. When children are fully received and accepted, and the light of the

mother and the family are available to them, they are more
likely to feel as if they truly belong in this unfamiliar
world.

During the first six months of pregnancy, your primary
focus is to join your Seed of Light with your child's Seed,
which builds a strong foundation between you. Your two
fields merge and blend, creating tenderness and softness.
You can feel the nature of your unborn child and be in
touch with your own nature. It is not just love that binds
you together, but a steadily growing awareness and
connection.

Flow Light Through Your Body

1. Sit or stand quietly.

2. Take a few deep breaths.

3. Create the intention to fill your body with light.

4. Imagine a bright light flowing from the top of
   your head down through all the parts of your
   body.

5. Gently and steadily bathe yourself in light.

6. Anchor the light within the cells of your organs
   and physical systems.

7. Take a deep breath and let the visualization
   subside.

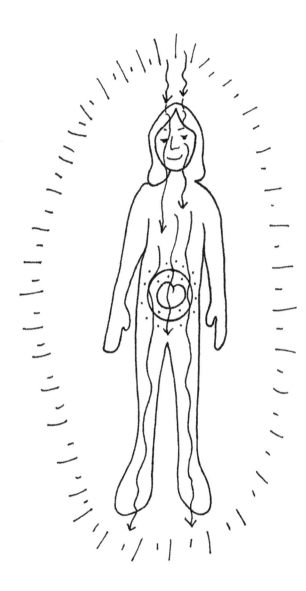

Flow Light Through Your Body

Filling yourself with light expands your energy field and brings greater health to your body. In the next exercise, you will bring light through you into your child's body.

Flow Light Through Your Child's Body

1. Sit quietly.

2. Take a few deep breaths.

3. Create the intention to fill your child's body with light.

4. Visualize the body of your child as it is curled within you.

5. Imagine light flowing down from the top of your head and into your womb as you cradle your child with your arms and hands.

6. Imagine that there is a bright light flowing from the top of the child's head through all parts of its body.

7. Gently and steadily, bathe the child in light.

8. Anchor the light within the cells of your child's organs and physical systems.

9. Take a deep breath and let the visualization subside.

Flow Light Through Your Child's Body

Bring light from the top of your head down through your body every day. Breathing in light can help you relax and keep your energy flowing more evenly. Since you are an energy system, bringing light through your body stabilizes you and grounds your life force, helping you relax and be more sensitive to the messages your body is sending you.

Suggested Daily Practice

- Imagine a column of light flowing like a shower through your body.

- Become aware of your breath. Practice breathing in and out, slowly and deeply. If you are uncomfortable or anxious, breathing in this way will help. It will also prepare you for your birthing experience. Build confidence in your ability to slow down and become calm.

- Flow the column of light for about 10-15 minutes, perhaps before sleep and upon awakening.

- When you use light daily to sustain your connection with your child and communicate with your body, you have a deeper sense of what is happening. How is your pregnancy affecting your body? How can you be more present for yourself and your baby? What would assist you to be more confident and more prepared for the process of birth?

Chapter Nine

Creating a Welcoming Space

Sometime during your pregnancy, you might want to create a very special place just for your unborn child. It might be in the nursery or another place in the home. Some parents create an altar (a sacred place) where they put things that have special meaning. Candles, flowers, pictures of the family and pets, notes, poems, letters, and drawings are just a few things that can be put in this place to welcome your child to your family. Use the altar in any way that you wish. Bringing the sacred into everyday life feels good and makes our experiences more meaningful.

To create a welcoming space inside your womb, use toning, singing and chanting. These methods send a vibration to your unborn child which strengthens your connection.

(Visit the Appendix, page 83, to learn about the importance of using sound to send encouragement and loving feelings to create a bridge in your shared field. Sound also assists you to deepen breathing and to tone your body in preparation for delivery.)

Chapter Ten

Six Weeks Before Birth

Let us review for a moment the exercises and experiences that you are creating: you are communicating with your baby through your Seeds of Light; you are connecting with your child's energy field and sharing impressions, sensations, and information; every day you are showering your body with light and singing to your child.

At about six weeks before your due date, if you have a good idea of what the circumstances of the birth will be, you can:

- Show your child the environment where he will be born and the people you expect to be there. If possible, go to the hospital or birthing center where the delivery will occur. You might show him the room, the bed, the lights in the ceiling, and the colors of the walls. If he will be born at home, show him the room you are preparing for his birth. It may be wise to show all the possibilities to prepare for any eventuality.

- Who will be there? Will he be suctioned to help him breathe? Will he be dried with a scratchy cloth? Will he be placed in your arms right away? Will he be separated from you for a while? How long will you be in this place?

- Ask your child what he wants during the delivery. Does he want a quiet environment? Low light? Music? Family members nearby? Be aware of your child's sensibilities and choices. Accommodate his wishes as best you can. If you can't do so, explain the circumstances, let him know that you are doing your best, and work together on a solution.

The intention for pre-birth sharing is to decrease anxiety and increase communication between you, your child, and your family. It can also reduce the child's feeling of being lost or separate from you, which is inevitable as the umbilical cord is cut. Prepare him for this experience. Let him know that as part of his growth, he will stand by himself, but his spirit, your spirit, and the spirits of the people who love him will remain connected in the field you share together. His identity is honored in this fabric of life, and he does not need to feel alone.

Let him know that your energy field will remain around you, and that his energy field will remain around him. At birth your two physical bodies will separate, but your connection with each other will remain through the energy field that you share. Knowing that there is really no separation instills in your child an understanding of where he fits in the world to which he is born.

Connection
and
Communication
During the Birth

Chapter Eleven

The Birth

Continue to experience a daily connection with your child, your body, and your energy system. When signs of labor begin, communicate more intently with your baby. Feel the excitement, the quickening that you share. The moment of birth is about to happen! Sense how this is for your child, and let her know how it is for you. Keep the connection between you as clear as you can so that you can sense anything she needs. You may also say birthing prayers or affirm that "you are light" during delivery to maintain connection and communication.

As contractions begin, your water breaks, or pressure increases, share your responses with your child and with those around you. You might experience a rush of energy in your body at some point right before delivery. Remember to breathe deeply in and out as the delivery becomes imminent. Steady yourself.

Keep the connection with your child as strong as you can, but at this point, ask your husband, partner or someone who knows you well to send light through your womb and birth canal as the delivery proceeds. You may be unable to focus as intently from here on in, and since the child responds to thoughts and intentions, someone close to you and the baby can help the child come into the world on a chute of light.

Have your helper:

- Bring light down through your body by imagining a shower of light coming from the top of your head, through your body, and out through your birth canal.

- Affirm that you are light and spirit, out loud or to themselves. ("You are light. You are spirit.")

(See Appendix, page 75, for Teresa Robertson's "Signal Exercise")

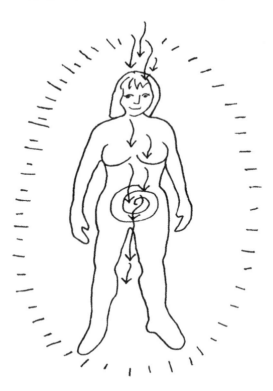

The Birthing

Chapter Twelve

Pay Attention to Your Body's Knowing

During the birth process, you will be receiving instructions from your midwife, doula (birthing helper), doctor, nurses or naturopath. At the same time, be sure to pay close attention to your *own* awareness of your body, your child, and the way you sense the birth is going. *Trust your inherent wisdom as the mother of your child* as it becomes necessary to make decisions during the delivery. Invite your knowing to come forth as you breathe the life of your child into being.

No matter what happens during the birth, do your best to stay as relaxed as possible. This tends to make the whole process easier. If you want to talk, sing, grunt, or yell, go for it! This is your time, so be natural. You can call on your ancestors to help you. You can open to embrace all mother-wisdom at this time, simply by breathing deeply and asking for assistance. As women, we are connected to the ancient feminine, which is very powerful. Your cells hold wisdom that is available when you ground your life force energy through your breath and intention.

Chapter Thirteen

Unexpected Possibilities and Cesarean Delivery

Your months of connection and preparation will make it easier to be present with whatever unfolds during the birthing process. Decisions and challenges can be handled more easily because you have established bonds between you, your child, and those who accompany you during the birth. You are ready to stay more calm because you are strongly connected with yourself and with your child.

If birth complications arise, such as a long or protracted birth, or if there is a need for surgical intervention such as a Cesarean delivery, keep the communication with your child strong. You may receive impressions about what is happening, what is needed, or how you can help make this an easier experience for both of you. At times like these, split-second decisions may be necessary.

Before labor begins, create an intention with your child that no matter what your state of consciousness, you will stay connected. You might create a key word such as "love" to keep your bond strong. One mother, who was under anesthesia during her baby's delivery, reported a profound mystical experience with her child.

You can also ask a health care provider, friend, or relative to say a prayer or affirmation for you that evokes light and helps to calm you during your experience.

Chapter Fourteen

At The Moment of Birth

At the moment of birth, in the blink of an eye, the newborn bonds with the mother on all levels: body-to-body, emotion-to-emotion, mind-to-mind, and spirit-to-spirit. The mother's fears, conditioning and past traumas are part of the patterns that the child inherits. Even though these patterns are not necessarily present for the child while in the womb, they can be imprinted on the newborn at birth. This is why it is important for the mother to clear her energy field with light as much as possible during pregnancy and delivery.

Bringing your child through the birth canal in light helps mediate and balance ancestral patterns and assists the child to be free from the mother's conditioning. The child has more freedom to be himself, which is a great gift.

After your child is born, there is a space or void in your womb. If you find yourself feeling empty, sad, or confused, don't worry. Continuing to fill your body with light helps you adjust. Since you and your child have been as one for nine months, it can take both of you some time to make the transition to experiencing yourselves as independent beings.

Honor Your Child As Light

1. The first time you hold your infant, or as soon after birth as possible, connect with her as you did before birth. Feel the energetic pathways between you. Intend that this new body and your body, this new soul and your soul, will find solace and peace together, no matter what your environment, what has happened, or what may lie ahead.

2. Affirm your child as light by placing her on your heart and saying in your mind or aloud,

    > You are light, and light you shall remain.
    > You are light, and light you shall remain.
    > You are light, and light you shall remain.

    Saying this three times imprints the affirmation into your infant's awareness.

3. The beauty of this message will help your baby relax. You are acknowledging that you remember your pre-birth communication, that your fields are still joined, and that the deep, sweet connection you formed will continue now that she is born. You are assuring her that you honor her as a spiritual being.

Honoring and Welcoming
Your Child

Chapter Fifteen

The First 48 Hours

An energetic channel is opened to make birthing possible, and as a new mother, you are more open for the first two days after giving birth than at any other time in your life. It is a very important time for you to feel connected with your spirit. During the first 48 hours, especially, be aware of your energy field and imagine it flowing. Breathe deeply and fill your body with light. Do this several times a day.

Since a friendly hubbub is common during the first few days, you might need to make a strong intention to take care of yourself in this way. Whether you are in the hospital, at a birthing center, or at home, family and friends may be dropping by, wishing you well and greeting your newborn.

You may have to tell them that you need some time alone to focus on being as clear and centered as you can be. Your family and friends will very likely understand this and respect your need for quiet time for yourself and for your baby. Remember that it is your right to do this. The quality of your connection during these first few days is very important to you and your infant.

Chapter Sixteen

Soul-To-Soul Bonding

To continue your connection with the soul of your child, you can join your Seeds of Light just as you did prior to his birth. You can link your souls when you pick him up, when you change his diaper, when you feed him—any time you think of it. He will feel this bond deep within him and know that he is safe in the world. Soul bonding is a shared ritual that you can experience in different forms and contexts for the rest of your lives. It is a way to stay bonded, even when events or situations in your lives are challenging.

Bonding through the fabric of the soul, because it is without words, offers us a deeply sensitive way to be heard, acknowledged and understood during times when we are feeling disconnected or upset. Because the bond between you is strong, it offers space for resting and accepting each other.

When your child is hungry, tired, or upset, send a golden thread over to his soul and bring it back to yours, reinforcing the connection. Experiment with this method of communication, noticing his response. You may find that it calms you and relaxes him.

Soul-to-Soul Bonding

1. Hold your child in your arms.

2. Take a few deep breaths and feel gratitude that you are holding your child.

3. Create an intention to bond with him as you did when he was in the womb.

4. Focus on your soul space just below your heart.

5. Imagine light coming out from that space as an arc.

6. Send this light to connect with your child's soul in the same location in his body, underneath the rib cage.

7. Bring the light back into you so that you are making a figure 8 as a golden ray of light between you, blending together.

8. Let his energy guide your energy. (Newborns are still floating in the spiritual dimension. Allow him to take you into a meditation where you are floating also. This can be a beautiful experience for both of you.)

9. Lie or sit together as long as you are comfortable and undisturbed.

10. Gently let the visualization subside.

11. Anchor this experience by doing whatever is natural in the moment. Smile, coo, sing, hold your child to your heart, etc.

Chapter Seventeen

Rituals For the Newborn

Congratulations! You have brought forth the gift of life! Take a deep breath. Feel the light that you carry within you. Give thanks for this profound experience and for the child you have brought into the world.

Bring Light Through Your Baby's Body

As soon as you can, hold her feet and draw light in through the top of her head like a shower, just as you drew light through your own head, body, and birth canal. Bring light from her head all the way through her torso and legs and out the bottoms of her feet. Direct the light and energy to flow smoothly through her body.

Much of the discomfort that babies express physically or emotionally stems from the fact that they have not yet adjusted to being in a physical form. Perhaps the light hasn't fully entered their bodies or isn't connected all the way through the bottoms of their feet. Being bathed in light and having a smooth energy flow can reduce or prevent conditions such as colic, sleeplessness, and irritability, and assists in maintaining a healthy immune system.

One grandmother tells the story of her granddaughter's birth. Since the child was delivered surgically, the grandmother was not able to be with her daughter or see her grandchild until she was brought into the nursery. Family members watched through the glass window as the nurses cleaned up the baby and checked her vital signs. The child was crying loudly during the whole process. The grandmother was longing to touch her granddaughter. However, since only one family member could be with the child at a time, and the baby's father was with her, the grandmother had to wait. Finally she was allowed into the nursery. She took her granddaughter's tiny feet in her hands, held them, and said softly to the little one, "You are light, and light you shall remain. You are light, and light you shall remain. You are light, and light you shall remain. Welcome to earth and to our family." The child's small body immediately relaxed and she stopped crying.

Bring the stream of light through your child several times a day. Hold her feet as you do this. The feet are the body's anchor to the earth, and you want her to feel at home here. You want her spirit, emotion, mind, and body to be fully present. Bringing light through will assist in this integration. (A good time to do this is when you are changing her diaper.)

Blessing Your Child (The Birthing Prayer)

Shortly after the birth, or whenever it is quiet and appropriate, gather those who would like to participate in the blessing of your child. Included could be the parents, siblings, grandparents, friends, etc. The mother, who is representing the whole family, places one hand on the heart of the child and the other hand on her heart and says:

You are light and I honor you.

You have come to this place to live with me.

*I know that you are from me and
that I do not in any way own you.*

You are free.

You are a child of light, a child of the universe.

*I know you have wisdom and truth within you,
and I honor that wisdom and truth.*

I give you permission to live your own truth.

*I ask you to respect my truth,
but I will not ask you to live my truth.*

Your truth is yours, and my truth is mine.

*Your ability to know is deep and profound,
and I respect and honor it.*

*I will guide you, but I will not expect you to
live my life or my ways.*

*I will always encourage and support your creativity and
the fulfillment of your potential.*

*In every way I will be open to the experiences you have,
always loving you from my soul, always understanding
that our love will continue for all time.*

*There is nothing you have to do to win my love.
There is no condition or situation upon which I will
remove my love from you.*

*I will love you forever,
and that is promised to you in this moment.*

This blessing is a profound way to honor your child. You are speaking from your heart and giving your child permission to live from the Seed of Light within her soul. You are calling her potential into being and pledging to always honor her wisdom. You are telling her that she does not have to believe what you believe, and you will not make her give up her wisdom for yours. She will not have to give up her truth for yours, while also honoring yours. These affirmations form the basis of the respect that you will sustain between you.

As your child grows, one of the things that will mean the most to her is that she doesn't have to give herself up to love you or to be loved by you. She doesn't have to change who she is to be successful in the world or to be loved by others.

Tell your child that you will work things out together. Let her know that in your family system, love is unconditional. You will *always* love her, no matter what she does. Of course, you will not give her permission to do just anything, or to disrespect you, but it does let her know that you will never withdraw your love from her.

This blessing is not only for newborns. It can be offered to anyone—other children, adults, grandparents, and friends. You may want to say it at birthdays and other important times, or include it in sacred ceremonies that you create.

Acknowledge Your Child's Spirit

During the first two days after birth, or soon thereafter, speak the affirmations below to your child. They are designed to honor and acknowledge her spirit. With each sentence, send a picture in your imagination to convey the meaning of what you are saying. Consciously hold your child in your energy field, just as you do when you are bonding.

Before you begin, bring light through the top of your head, through your body, and all the way through your feet to clear your energy field and to be as present as possible.

**Look into your child's eyes or
speak into her ear, and say quietly:**

I come to you in spirit.

I acknowledge your divinity and your spirit.

You have arrived on earth.

*There are many rules here, but the most
important rule in our family is that we are divine,
that we are loved completely at all times by each other,
for each other, and through each other.*

*You are always creative and can
accomplish anything you desire.*

*There are no conditions on my love for you,
absolutely no conditions on my love for you.*

Hold the bottoms of her feet and say:

You have chosen to come into form.
You have chosen to come into form.
You have chosen to come into form.

I anchor you into the Mother Earth.
I anchor you into the Mother Earth.
I anchor you into the Mother Earth.

Now say again:

You are light, and light you shall remain.
You are light, and light you shall remain.
You are light, and light you shall remain.

When you say this, she will experience the circle of life.

Put one hand on her heart and say three times:

The link that we have is through love.

What I teach you, I teach from love.

What is not compatible with your truth,
I give you permission to release.

When you run light through her body, affirm who she is, and ground her to the earth, you are helping her feel that the world is a safe place to be.

(Visit the Appendix, page 101, and read the entire birthing chapter at this point.)

Infant Massage

Infant massage is another easy way to help your child be comfortable in her body, and it also deepens your bond. The soothing massage helps your child relax just before bedtime. The physical and emotional benefits of infant massage are well-documented.

(Visit the Appendix, page 97, for more on Infant Massage.)

Chapter Eighteen

The Fields of Interconnection

The need for security is basic to human growth. One way that we feel safe is through our connection with others. If we perceive our energy fields and the energy fields of others as joined, we can feel connection, acceptance, love, co-creation, sharing, and a sense of belonging. If we perceive our energy fields as separate, we can feel rejection, loss, separation, grief, detachment or anger. Though this feeling of connection or separation is not verbal, it is very real. Our relationship with others and how we perceive this relationship shapes our sense of self and determines whether we feel included or excluded from life's events and whether we feel safe or unsafe.

Through the intention to love and cherish your child, you established a conscious connection with him before birth. Your fields were joined when he was in your womb, and you both felt safely held on a deep level. There were no conditions or requirements. It is very different after the birth. Now there are demands on your time and energy. There are feeding schedules and diapers to change. You may not be getting enough sleep. Things are new for both of you as you learn to connect in a different way. However, remember that you have already set the foundation for connection and communication with your child, and you can build upon this as he grows.

Continuing to develop an understanding of the relationship between your field and the field of your newborn can make this adjustment easier. You can prepare him for experiences and people he will encounter in his immediate environment by sending him pictures. You can let him know, through remembering your own experiences, that some situations seem to be harder than others, and that one can stay connected to others and to oneself, even when outer events are challenging.

When you identify the energy field patterns that you have with others and you have an awareness of how these patterns work, you can communicate this nonverbally to your child. You might first identify those people with whom you have a comfortable pattern. Then identify those with whom you experience challenges.

One way to identify patterns is to use your imagination to show the child pictures of his energy field, your field, and the fields of those you live with. You can do this just as you showed him the faces of those he would meet before he was born. Show him how configurations change during different situations.

It is very helpful for you to identify your energy field patterns and those of your parents. Many times these patterns are repeated over and over, from generation to generation. It is also possible that roles such as victim or perpetrator are actual "field-like" patterns that continue from parent to child. Recognizing the patterns that exist in your family can assist you to make choices that allow you to change unhealthy behaviors, foster independence, and provide new relationships built on love and mutual respect. Your understanding of these patterns can be communicated to your child.

This simple exercise can offer information about how you are affected by intimacy, challenge, power, self-esteem, sexual connection, competition, or jealousy. Who is too close to you? Who is too far away? How does changing the relationship with this space make you feel better or worse? Identifying the space and content of your fields allows for a new response to be experienced in your body.

Circle Exercise:
Identifying Family Energy Field Patterns

1. Draw yourself and others in your family as separate circles.

2. Cut out the circles and move them around. For example, put your significant other's circle above or behind yours. How does that feel? Move his or her circle next to yours. Does that feel different? Move the person's circle to the other side of you. Does that change anything? How do you feel when you are near him or her in the new configuration? How do you feel when you are near other people in your life? Try to be aware of what is causing comfort or discomfort when you are near certain people.

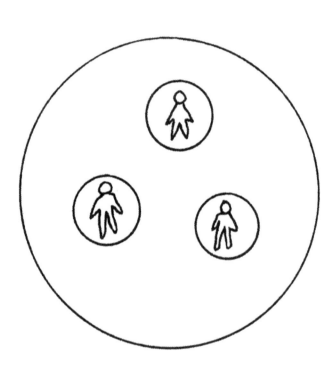

Separate Fields

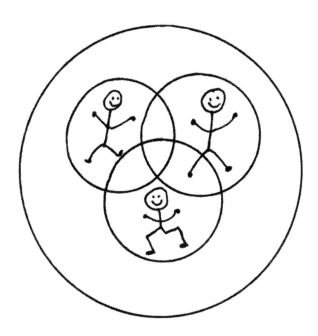

Connected Fields

Identifying Patterns of Interconnection

1. Sit quietly.

2. Take three or four deep breaths.

3. First, reflect on those people who are close to you and live in your home. Knowing that each of these people has an individual field, draw their field. (Work with one circle for each person at a time to identify their patterns and the relationship of those patterns to your pattern.)

4. How do their fields and yours connect when you are comfortable? How does the field change when you are uncomfortable?

5. Are there patterns that seem evident in your family history that might explain your discomfort? Are there patterns that may be repeated as family members relate with your newborn child?

6. Notice the distance or closeness of your fields and what affects this proximity.

7. Breathe and feel as centered, calm, and connected as you can to your Seed of Light. Do you experience a difference in how you perceive your spatial relationship or individual life field when you are more connected with yourself? Is there a change in the fields of others when you are more centered?

8. As you observe where each person is in the family field (close here, farther apart there),

how do you feel? If you would like to affect these patterns for yourself, your child, or your family, you can use imagination, inner sight, intuitive sensing, or your body's feeling to shift the position of individuals and their fields. As you relax and breathe, move the people and see their fields relate from this new place. Notice the potential for improving family dynamics as the fields relate in a healthy and balanced way with each other.

9. Take a deep breath and let the visualization subside. You might want to write down what you experienced.

This exercise provides an opportunity to change the interpersonal dynamics in your family or any human system. It also builds on the first circle exercise.

Knowing that unity and connection are fostered energetically provides a map for you, your child, and your family. This map describes your relationships and your actions and helps make sense out of patterns and tendencies that show up in your world. Understanding how your family's field relationships have been established and how they operate provides a guidance system for problem solving. When a child learns that an adjustment in his field is possible, this brings an autonomy that fosters independence, confidence, and self-assurance.

Show him how feeling alone can be changed by consciously joining fields with someone else, or remembering when his fields were joined with others, with a pet, a tree, a person, etc.

Teach him that all fields are really connected all of the time. Everyone belongs to a huge tribal family. Having this experience sustains the field of the child and helps him understand more about how family and social dynamics occur.

The family can create a field where there is respect and acceptance. This offers respite to all members of the family and support to each person simultaneously. In a unified field, each person is valued and there is recognition that everyone plays a vital role and is equally important. It is understood by all family members that nonverbal communication is important to personal security. When those who guide a child provide him with this security, there is a basis for understanding that he has a place here, and then the fullness of life's potential is brought into the very center of his world.

When we foster and sustain a child's essence without condition or expectations, we uphold her life and nurture her purpose. Together, we can sing a new song of harmony and co-creation—a song that upholds and honors each person. Together, we can bring the promise of each child to its fullest fruition.

Thank you for choosing to nurture the gift of your child's life and spirit.

Appendix

Communicating With Your Unborn Child
Teresa Robertson, RN, Certified Nurse Midwife, MS

Signal Exercise

It is helpful to establish a quick method for your baby to get your attention. In this exercise, you will talk to the baby about creating two levels of signals. One is for every day, and one is a 911. These signals can also be used after the baby is born as a continued way to remain connected and aware of each other's needs.

Regular Signal

This one is used when your baby desires your attention. Perhaps he wants you to slow down, or connect with him, or buy some broccoli for dinner.

1. Ground by bringing light through your body and feet into the earth.

2. Establish communication with your baby.

3. Ask for a signal to get your attention. This might be a bodily feeling such as a kick or a feeling of pressure in your shoulder.

4. Wait, listen, and see what comes. You will get a sense of what your baby wants you to do.

---

911 Signal

Originally, I created the 911 signal for my home birth clients as a way to seek help.

The 911 is to be used only when the baby needs you to connect with your health care practitioner. To obtain the signal:

1. Ground yourself.

2. Establish communication with your baby.

3. Ask for a 911 signal. Unlike the regular signal, the 911 should not be a bodily sensation. I often suggest something like seeing flashing lights or hearing bells or sirens.

4. Wait, listen, and see what comes.

For parents, your part of the agreement is to seek help and not go into fear when the baby elicits the signal. The baby's end of this agreement is to use it only when it needs help, and to give you enough time to safely obtain it.

In the world of obstetrics, practitioners have great respect for listening to moms when they come in saying, "Something doesn't feel right. I am worried about the baby." It is my experience that they will check you out and not think you are crazy.

I have had parents attune to this signal, then go safely to get their own needs and their babies' health needs attended to.

I have also had this signal work for me. For example, if I am driving at night on a curvy, dangerous canyon road and "see" flashing lights (my 911 signal), I invariably slow down to find an accident or wildlife in the middle of the road.

Nourishment Exercise

I have been sharing the following exercise with pregnant women for fifteen years. It is also a fun exercise to do with the other parent. It has found its way into my life when my body is hungry for something, or if I am ill. I just ask, and I get answers.

Don't become confused if the baby asks you to avoid things you are already avoiding. (Examples: coffee, alcohol, sugar.) Use that as a validation for doing a great job!

Nourishment Exercise

1. Connect with your baby.

2. Ask, "Where is your energy going? What parts of you are you developing?"

3. Be aware of what you may see, feel, know, hear, or smell.

4. Ask the baby:

    *   What foods can I bring into my system to assist you with growing (for example) your hair, hands, stomach?

    *   Which foods should I avoid?

    *   What drink/supplements would you like me to add? to avoid?

    *   What activities would be helpful to do?

    *   What activities should I be avoiding?

    Remember that napping, making love, and massage are all considered activities.

Receiving a Healing From Your Baby

Since our babies reside in the world of spirit, they can offer amazing healing perspectives. Many parents think they should not receive healing from their child. After all, they are the parent and should be taking care of their baby!

The truth is, many babies love to work on their parents. Being aware of the parents' needs qualifies the baby spirit as a perceptive and effective healer. An unborn baby has a unique and powerful position to help prepare your body for conception or for the process of giving birth.

In this process, it is essential that there be clear boundaries. It is important that the baby spirit has a boundary (a bubble around itself) and that you have your boundary (a bubble around you). Babies work very quickly and are usually done within a minute or two.

Receiving a Healing From Your Baby

1. Connect with your baby. Ask if he or she feels if it would be beneficial for you to receive a healing.

2. Ground your body.

3. Establish boundaries between your baby and you.

4. Relax and be open to the baby spirit working.

5. As the baby works on you, you may feel warmth, a vibration, an excited feeling, receive the answer to a yes or no question, or see something. Commonly, during their first experiences, parents feel warmth, relaxation, or a buzzing sensation. If an image or communication is not clear, ask the baby to share the answer with you in a manner which you can understand.

6. Ask the baby for a clear signal when he/she is done. Thank your child for the healing, and acknowledge that it is complete.

Giving Your Baby Healing

You can offer to give your baby a healing, which is essentially an energy sponge bath in-utero.

Giving Your Baby Healing

1. Ask the baby if he/she would like a healing. Good times to check in with the baby are after exposure to ultrasound, a loud noise, or an intense situation or emotion you may have experienced. Remember that the Doppler used to listen to your baby's heartbeat is an ultrasound device.

2. Ground yourself and establish your boundaries with your child.

3. Ask the baby what color and concept it would like in the sponge bath. (Examples are calm & vitality for concepts, and blue/gold for colors.)

4. Ascertain with the baby where it would like you to start gently sponging it. Inside the womb? the placenta? from head to toe? toe to head? the belly?

5. Maintain your connection with your baby. Be aware of any signals from your child to slow down, change the activity, or stop.

6. Ask your baby for a clear signal when the sponge bath is complete and acknowledge the completion of the healing.

Teresa Robertson RN, Certified Nurse Midwife, MS, Birth Intuitive, provides information, support and tools to assist her clients to connect with their unborn children. She is a translator between the worlds of intuition and western allopathic medical approaches.

Her work aids clients: to promote fertility; to heal and to resolve pregnancy losses such as miscarriage and abortion; to heal and/or minimize pregnancy complications; and to assist adoptive parents in connecting with their unborn children.

Information about her services are on her Website, www.Birthintuitive.com.

Welcoming Babies With Song
Giselle E. Whitwell, MT- BC, Birth Doula

There are many myths from distant cultures and peoples regarding the creation of the world through sound, indicating that coming into being is a sonorous event. Sound has been used in almost all places and time periods as the means for transforming matter back into spirit as well as manifesting matter physically with sound.

Ideally, music in its various forms should be an early companion during the time of pregnancy. Some women, finding themselves pregnant for the first time, suffer from stress and anxiety about their condition, the impending labor and delivery, as well as their changing role as women and their new responsibilities. Sound and music can become a joyous healing ally during this time, also bringing spiritual awareness through this process. Communication with the unborn child is then a more holistic experience. It is deep spiritual, affective, primordial and intimate contact.

During gestation the communication through sound is one of the most basic and important links between a mother and her child. Through song and words she nurtures and stimulates her baby physically, emotionally, mentally and spiritually. In so doing, the mother reveals to the child who she is and her qualities, as the baby is enveloped in her sound environment, whether she is conscious of it or not. All of her feelings and thoughts are transmitted to the baby while in her womb. There are no secrets she can keep from her child, for she is an open book.

From this unique communication the baby draws emotional sustenance and begins to form his psyche. It is through the quality of this first relationship that the baby will continue to build subsequent relationships and patterns of communication.

The baby in the womb perceives not only the spoken word and sounds around him, but also senses the unspoken thoughts and feelings of the mother in particular—the whole environment that surrounds him. As conscious parents, we can live so that our inner world is in harmony with the outside reality, and thus nurture wholeness.

Sound, song and language are intimately connected from our earliest development in the womb. This begins with the developing sense of hearing, a sense that is fully formed before birth, in size and function, though it continues to refine afterwards. The faculty of hearing is one of the most important senses, providing a dual function. The cochlea system of the ear, which processes frequencies of sound, also energizes the brain through the higher frequencies of speech and song, whereas the vestibular system of the ear is actively involved with our sense of balance and movement in general.

The ear first appears in the 3rd week of gestation and it becomes functional by the 16th week. The baby in the womb begins active listening by the 24th week. We know from ultrasound observations that babies hear and respond to a sound pulse starting about 16 weeks of age; this is even before the ear structure is completely developed. There is more to hearing than the physical development of the ear alone. The sense of hearing develops gradually, beginning first with skin sensing throughout the whole body, then the vestibular system emerges and lastly the cochlea.

Hearing for the baby is predominantly through bone and water conduction, both being excellent carriers of sound transmission. The inner ear or cochlea hears sound mostly through the bones surrounding the skull of the baby and the mother's bones. As a consequence, the mother's voice is a predominant sound in the womb. The baby lights up and listens for this voice because it is unlike anything else in his environment. The development of this part of hearing has the most dramatic impact because the baby develops emotional and relational dynamics with the mother. The baby begins to gather memories out of these sensory experiences and to establish his psychic life. Listening to the mother's voice is one of the most fundamental perceptions and forms the basis of the desire to communicate, which begins soon after conception.

The sound of the mother's voice is what creates a lasting influence on her baby. She embodies the sound that communicates to her baby a sense of well being, joy, excitement, relaxation, or fear, disinterest, not being wanted, etc. The baby is listening all the time. Even if the mother feels self-conscious about her voice or cannot carry a tune, she needs to know that babies carry no judgment. Her voice will always be regarded as a cherished gift. What matters is the feeling and the thoughts with which she approaches the communication, the bond that is forming as a consequence. Her voice carries love and beauty for her child. She does not have to be perfect, but just give her baby enough warmth/love to sustain the life that she is carrying in her womb.

Singing is possibly the most important activity for a pregnant mother. It weaves a harmonious tapestry through all parts of her being—the physical, emotional, mental and spiritual selves. Singing allows the mother to express her inner feelings, liberating her from inner tensions and reestablishing a sense of acceptance and peace. The body itself is a musical instrument through which we resonate to the world. Chinese medicine has assigned particular tones to each organ in our body. Singing not only stimulates the baby appropriately with positive qualities but also engages the mother in conscious bonding and parenting. Music and sound that is offered during the pregnancy is therefore very powerful and effective.

Music is an energy field, and when it begins to vibrate in our bodies, it gives us a sound massage. This in turn stimulates the baby in the womb, nurturing mother and child simultaneously with joy and well-being. The mother is consciously creating for her child the reality of the now and the future. Matter is being formed within the mother for the baby she is carrying when she sings and tones. Music used pre-natally sets a particular harmony for the new life to come. I believe that music in this way supports the descent of spirit into matter.

Mother and child may experience an authentic symbiosis, in which case the mother vibrates at the same frequency as her child. The baby forms a bond with his mother from the beginning of his existence; the mother's bond on the other hand may take time to evolve and is not necessarily an automatic event. When there is a loving and ongoing communication established between them the baby will develop a positive worldview. It is the qualities that are sustained in this relationship that are the seeds which will ultimately influence whether life is a joyous or stressful experience, whether one is wanted or merely tolerated; from these premises all future psychological and emotional tendencies will arise.

We begin the practice by always tuning ourselves into our innermost being, where we have access to our soul and spirit. We sit first in silence, becoming conscious of our breath, and then with an exhalation we allow the sound to emerge with any vowel. After a while we can extend the inner qualities experienced to where they need to manifest, whether in our physical selves or as an offering to the being who is incarnating. It can likewise manifest in song or toning. This is a way to commune with her baby, and to sense her needs, to reassure her, to develop her own intuition, to be in touch with her whole being and that of her baby. This kind of attunement approaches a harmonious state of being. Singing daily brings joy and harmony not only to oneself but also to all that which surrounds us.

Deep and slow breathing is a necessary foundation for any vocalization. A calm, rhythmic and deep breath is the basis in which sound can manifest harmoniously. This means breathing with the lower, middle and upper lung. It is a conscious act full of reverence, gratitude and love for receiving the benefits contained in the air. Breathing is receiving nurturing elements for body and soul from the universe, sometimes referred to as *life forces*. We start life with an inhalation and leave this earth with an exhalation, the cycle comes full circle to complete itself. Breath, sound, voice, language, and communication are all wondrously interwoven in the beginning of our life, so that we can evolve into a greater sense of our humanity.

The voice, according to Hazrat Inayat Khan, is the expression of man's spirit. The voice is not only audible but also visible to those who can see it. This fact was well known in the ancient world where it was thought that singing is the first art, playing an instrument the second art and dancing the third art. The Hindus believed that the shortest way to achieve spiritual enlightenment was by singing.

The voice is as extension of our inner self that meets the

world. As mothers free their voices before birth, their journey can flow in harmony. It is the path of the heart, because through sound we experience our feelings. Heartfelt devotion nurtures mother and child. The voice is a good barometer of our physical, emotional, mental and transcendent well-being. Furthermore, because of the power of resonance through the voice, one can heal oneself. Our voice is an exquisite, powerful, undervalued, and unconscious instrument, which needs to be awakened from its hibernating state.

If we choose to sing, tone, chant and listen to our own voice, we will discover our true identity. Our intuition will emerge and guide us through our individual journeys. When we are in tune with our inner being then we have access to the power of healing and perceive a larger cosmos. The body through sound can vibrate every atom within itself, balancing all aspects of our being. While training our voice and ears, we will also learn how to breathe. Our life experiences will be recorded in our voice. We can't hide behind its mask; our voice will give us away, for it does not know how to lie. We have to have the courage to face ourselves. Finding that tone always gives us far more than we expect.

Singing *lullabies* is a missing link in our culture, a tradition that has been lost, and a spiritual connection that has been obliterated. We now have the opportunity to re-discover this tradition with new vitality and purpose for generations to come.

When a mother sings a lullaby to her child, it is one of the most important gifts she can give to her baby. Through these songs, mothers and fathers can convey their love, caring and welcome. Parents can compose their own lullabies, birthing songs, welcoming songs, etc. When sung before birth, these songs will form a bridge from the blissful womb life into their new surroundings. The songs will help babies with the adjustment period of the first three months after birth, and have a comforting effect if the baby suffers from colic or has complications. These lullabies form a familiar and natural environment that is recognized and therefore has a calming effect.

The heart as mediator of heaven and earth can thus manifest in spirit through the lullabies mothers sing to their babies. Singing from the heart builds intimate and personal relationships which I have personally witnessed between partners and close relatives. In the act of singing lullabies, the voices share themselves and join together into one sound, and the voice is then experienced as a union of feelings, a sense of oneness within oneself and with the cosmos at large. The lullabies then work silently to re-establish harmony and joy, beauty and peace.

Singing together with one's partner opens other avenues of communication, developing qualities that were not fully present before, a trust of one another and an expanding warmth of love. When the heart is nurtured we can bring social awareness and create a better world by perceiving the needs of others. In this sense singing lullabies together with one's partner or a larger group of pregnant couples fulfills an important social aspect.

In the experience of conscious singing or speaking, one is able to feel more intimately one's spiritual nature. Through the lullabies and chants the mother is able to discover in herself a selfless love and deep tenderness for the being she is carrying, a growing consciousness of the other. It is vital therefore that mothers-to-be consciously awaken this warmth element in themselves, which is em- bodied in the heart, so that they can draw from it during their pregnancy, birth and delivery as well as the most challenging time right after birth.

The mother who rejects her child or is indifferent will sow seeds of psychic damage or wounding. Babies develop memory during gestation. The experiences of the nine months of gestation are cumulative and are imprinted in their personalities and will manifest sooner or later in life.

Healthy bonding takes place through affectionate contact, loving presence, touch and sound during gestation. There are many ways in which this relationship can be developed. Parents may sing, dance, recite poetry, improvise on instruments, etc. However it manifests, it needs to be guided by love and playfulness. The father has the advantage of being able to sing right onto the skin of the mother's belly, like a drum. Babies also recognize their father's voice if he communicates on a regular basis. The father may also bond consciously with his child as early as possible. His voice will become familiar and be recognized at birth just like the mother's. It also provides him with an opportunity to create and sing his own particular songs and rhythms to calm a colicky baby.

The quality and choice of music during pregnancy has a great impact. Exposing babies to inappropriate music, such as music that is loud, percussive and with a monotonous rhythm as is found in rock and rap, can affect not only a baby's spiritual body, but also their developing physiology. Live music sung by the mother and father is the best possible choice. Mothers may sing their favorite lullabies while holding their abdomen and gently rocking or swaying, patting or tapping their belly on the beat of the music.

Prenatal listening recordings would be best from the

classical period of music including some Baroque and Renaissance music, particularly the slow movements or Adagios. That is the music closest to one's heartbeat, which is roughly between 65 and 80 beats per minute. When listening one needs to be mindful that not only that the ear is functioning, but that the whole body is listening. As music penetrates our whole being, it is an active engagement with focus and attention.

Songs that are heard consistently for a period of time before birth will be remembered for a lifetime. The songs can include sacred chants, lullabies and birthing songs. They will form a spiritual bridge as babies descend from celestial realms to the earthly plane and will help make the transition in ways that support our true humanity.

In some of the exercises offered in this book such as "The Seed of Light" or "Communicating With Your Unborn Child," one will begin to perceive the being who is incarnating, and maybe some unspoken qualities will emerge which can become the source of inspiration to create a welcoming song or a lullaby. Fathers can likewise participate in this way and offer a creative gift to their child. Let inspiration guide you along this path of creativity. Allow it to emerge without any judgment.

To sing with closed lips or *humming* is a related tradition to the lullabies. Mothers hum instinctively when their babies cry, as if they recognize the message within themselves. Humming may also have to do with its archetypal quality that reminds one of the universal mother.

Humming is an experience that is centered in the heart space, so the mother first tunes herself into this space, then feels the bond and connection to her baby. She may place her hands on her moon-belly and even move her hand around gently and softly in time with the chant or lullaby being hummed. A moment of silence afterwards is essential before concluding the experience. In this moment, one may sense a deeper feeling of oneness and bonding that lives in the stillness.

Toning is another voice practice recommended during pregnancy, labor and delivery. One extends the breath with sound on a single tone having a sustained and non-melodic quality. Toning during pregnancy and birth is using the voice to express sounds for the purpose of releasing tension, extending the breath and bringing extra oxygen into the body. This practice allows the mother to voice pain and joy, particularly in labor, provided it is done from deep-within-the-belly space.

Toning connects us to our intuitive self and energizes and relaxes, simultaneously. It will train the ears to listen qualitatively and more deeply. It has no detrimental effects such as screaming, which creates tension. It also allows the voice to become an instrument of self-expression, which we need in order to give birth in harmony with ourselves.

As we discover our own voice, we also learn its qualities, strengths and power. It is an instrument we can count on at all times. Toning with one's partner is very nurturing and bonding for all involved. Partners can sit back to back to feel the vibration. The father can tone directly on the mother's belly establishing communication with the baby. If done at regular intervals, the baby is likely to respond with a foot or a fist.

The quality of the sound however is most important. When the sound emerges from deep within the belly, the throat can remain relaxed and open. Women need to be able to moan, grunt, sigh, tone and sing during their pregnancy and especially while giving birth. In doing so they rejoice and give expression with all its nuances to the new life they are birthing. In labor, releasing sound while exhaling often helps to reduce the pain of intense contractions. Toning releases the vital force contained around one's energy field. I have witnessed this with women in labor. Through this practice, women become less inhibited using their voice.

The practice of toning, used consciously, may restore the vibratory pattern of the body to its perfect electro-magnetic field. The vowels are the vehicle used in toning. Through their resonance due to bone conduction, all internal organs are also energized. During pregnancy all vowels are practiced, but during the last weeks of pregnancy "o and u'" are most comforting. Through toning, the voice becomes a powerful instrument of trans-formation that is readily available at all times. The lower tones are more effective in relaxing tension. Toning is also comforting because one cannot make a mistake.

Toning offers many windows with which we can explore the unseen world of spirit. I find that toning takes you to an altered state of consciousness and offers opportunities for self-healing. The altered state includes daydreaming, pre-sleep states, and meditative consciousness as well as religious experiences. Toning has taught me to find in sound a sacred principle, a womb of sound that is ever present in the universe for us to tune into. It has also taught me the value of the spoken word—not to waste its gift by mindless chatter. As we discover our own voice, we also learn its qualities, strength and power.

In addition, prenatal singing and toning provides an opportunity for pregnant women to exercise their breathing muscles and develop the ability to exhale with a steady stream of air that increases relaxation, which is particularly important during labor.

Midwives have made us aware that the tightness in the jaw, throat and mouth affect the tension in the vaginal floor. Toning brings this awareness to the pregnant mother. By consciously relaxing the neck, jaw, throat and larynx one also achieves a sense of relaxation in the cervix. It follows the well-known spiritual principle "as above so below." Both organs, the larynx and the vagina, are our most creative organs.

Chanting is different than toning in that it includes simple melodies contained within a small range of tones with no meter and small musical intervals. Like in toning the exhalations are extended and therefore slow down the rate of breathing and blood pressure. One can experience a profound feeling of peace while chanting. Chanting is like a vocal meditation which has the ability to focus our attention in the moment. Like the other forms, whether singing or toning, chant also brings into balance our whole being— body, mind and soul. Chants come from a variety of sources and nationalities such as the Eastern Orthodox traditions (Bulgaria and Russia), Hindu and Sufi chants, Gregorian chant (Roman) and Hebrew.

Toning and chanting are very old musical forms of expression which are still valid and limitless in meeting the needs of today's pregnant mothers.

Affirmations can be used musically using a chant format. An affirmation is a positive thought or idea that one consciously focuses on in order to produce a desired result.

In my experience, toning, chanting, and singing during pregnancy and as preparation for labor and delivery effectively gives women a sense of responding in positive and creative ways to their experience. These musical forms become a creative act capable of expressing the pain and the joy of a culminating event in a woman's life, while at the same time supporting their altered state of consciousness and becoming a bridge from the spiritual realms.

A self-empowering music experience gives a sense of independence to the woman in labor, not requiring someone else to tell her what to do and when to do it, enhancing her self-confidence and self-esteem.

We are all living sound mandalas, each of us a kaleidoscope of ever-changing sound, dancing throughout the day between wellness and imbalance. We may not all see these sounding mandalas, but we certainly may feel them, as when we are in ecstasy or in pain. We foster a singing culture for our own well-being, for the evolution of humanity, and for parenting conscious future generations. Let us all begin and close each day with a song of gratitude and joy.

Since 1989 Giselle E. Whitwell has presented prenatal music themes at conferences world wide in Europe, South and North America, Asia and Russia. She has articles published in the Journal of Prenatal and Perinatal Psychology and Health, as well as in other journals and magazines.
Giselle established the Prenatal and Perinatal Music Center in Austin, Texas where she now practices and serves the community. Recently she has completed her certifications in Therapeutic Healing. She can be reached through email at prenatalmusic@yahoo.com or through her website at www.prenatalmusic.com.

From the Womb to the World
DeAnna Elliott

As babies come through the birth canal, they leave an environment that is dark, warm, liquid, and free of gravity to arrive in a world that is light, cold, dry, heavy, and often chaotic. Coming through the birth canal can also be trying for the child. Some infants are caught on the mother's pubic bone, making their entry into the world even more difficult. If this is the case, procedures are often used to assist the baby through the birth canal. Think for a moment about what this is like for babies that experience too much trauma in their birthing process.

In Western birthing practices, babies are usually taken away from the mother before the initial bonding can occur. Babies need help orienting to a completely new environment, and being held in the mother's arms just after birth helps them do this.

Infant Massage

Constructive touch from the parents during the first few hours of life can be a very effective way to encourage babies to relax into their bodies while at the same time releasing the traumas of birth. Infant Massage is a very effective tool for this process and has a positive impact on both infants and parents.

Infant Massage does a number of things to assist the baby with the transition from spirit into form. For example, the squeezing and stroking movements can bring the trauma of the child's entry up and out of the tissue to be released. Sometimes as this happens the child cries. Actually, these cries are good, for the babies are telling their "stories" to their parents of what their birthing process was like.

Even though it is difficult for parents to hear these cries, when they learn to listen to their babies and receive their stories, the little ones are so grateful because they need their parents, more than anyone else in the world, to hear their story. After they tell their story, their physical system relaxes and they often sleep for a very long time.

Physically, massage gives infants spatial-sequential orientation that is essential for learning. Psychologically, they learn where they start and stop and develop a rich understanding of their body. They begin to associate with their life and body, cope more easily with their birth trauma, and become present, which you can see in their eyes. They become confident in themselves and in what they can do.

Biologically, many things happen. Circulation is increased, sending more oxygen to all parts of the body. The colon evacuates more regularly, which removes toxins. Colic is reduced. Muscle groups become toned, and antibodies increase, as well as milinization of the nerve sheath. Endorphins are also released, which helps with deeper sleep.

When visualization is offered as well, the results are magnified. Some parents imagine light coming through their hands as they massage their infants. It is also helpful to imagine a light coming through the parent's body and merging with the light of the child in a field of love. The baby feels more peaceful, happy and connected, and so do the parents.

Because many mothers need to work soon after the baby is born, babies may be put in day care at an early age. Infant massage provides a special time with the child that can help compensate for eight hours apart. Mothers can come home, have dinner, give a bath, and massage the baby before bed. Incorporating infant massage into the daily schedule teaches parents to understand their child's body on new levels. Opening the tactile, kinesthetic channels between the parent and child opens new worlds of understanding and communication. They can feel when the child may be getting sick because the baby's body feels different when it is challenged physically.

We are experiencing more stress than ever before. Infants and children need stress management just as much as adults do. When babies receive a massage every day, they learn to understand their bodies, express compassion to others, develop a pre-disposition for a healthy constitution, and have higher self-esteem. Their stresses are released every day from their tissue, and this creates an imprint that says *you belong, you are whole, and you are loved.* The way a child is received at birth sets the foundation for the rest of its life. Infant massage helps provide a great beginning.

A good time to massage your baby is when he is warm, relaxed and happy, as after the bath before bedtime. The changing table works well for this. Use baby oil, almond oil or any gentle oil and massage for about five minutes.

1. Put a tiny bit of oil on your hands and rub them together until they are warm.
2. Gently stroke your baby's body. Start with the toes and work up the feet and legs to the torso.
3. Stroke the fingers and hands, moving up the arms to the shoulders.
4. Make *very* gentle clockwise circling movements on the baby's abdomen.

DeAnna Elliott began teaching Infant Massage certification in 1982 and offers trainings throughout the USA. She has seen many miracles in this work.

"Cellular Echoes, Environmental Influences in the Journey from the Womb to the World," is a documentary Deanna created about cellular imprinting from preconception into the early years. Tribal birth wisdom is compared to contemporary scientific information in an exploration of cellular imprinting.

You can learn more about DeAnna's work on her Website, www.foundationofglobalunity.org.

The Birthing

From *I Remember Union*

Flo Aeveia Magdalena

Mary Magdalene is speaking here of her journey to assist a mother who is about to give birth.

I rode swiftly, urging Saschai onward into the cool, damp darkness of the midnight sky, for I heard the calling in my mind and answered it.

There was one, a woman, coming into her time, and I must be there to assist her. The cycles and the rhythms of her birthing were unbalanced, and the body and the soul of the unborn child were, as yet, disconnected. If there was no one to bond the spirit to the body at birth, the soul would have no grounding place and would bind to the mother and to the patterns of man, and the beliefs of fear and judgment.

This was a special soul, one who would help to lead the people after I had gone, and it had been appointed that I attend it. I would teach it the ways of the Earth and reinforce the pathways of its calling, and that was why I must assist in its coming forth.

I was almost there. I could feel the energy of the coming, calling me forward. When I arrived, I took my pack from

Saschai and left her to graze, knocking upon the door frame of the small home before me.

The mother answered the knock, not appearing surprised to see me, relieved at my presence. She remarked that she was alone now. Her man, a shepherd, had gone with his flock, and she said it was good that I was there to be with her. She was older and seasoned, her face rich with experience and tempered with time, and this was her first birthing.

She invited me within and we sat in the way of women. I listened to her passage. She told me of the days of her life and the ways of her learnings, and I was aware of her fears and her strengthenings.

After a time she relaxed, telling me of her dreams, and then finally, of her saddenings. At times we laughed together, but always quietly and softly, as if honoring the presence of the unborn child through the whispers of our caring.

And after a time, when I knew that she was ready to listen to me, I told her of why I had come. I reached within me to the core of my memory and began to speak:

"There is a place called the Hierarchy where there is no hatred or fear or judgment, the place of the source, from which all souls are born. The truth is born with us from this space also; the truth of who we are and where we are from and why we have come here to learn. But we forget this.

"When we are born on the Earth, if those who birth us do not tell us this truth, we do not remember it. And therefore an amnesia is born and we feel separation from the truth and from the Gods. The ways of humankind, the greed, the fear, and the judgment, are because we do not remember that we are all from the same place, that we are all the same.

"The forgetting causes pain and then, after a time, the pain is expected. When the children are born, they are taught that the pain is a part of life, and that the separation is a part of life, and the competition and the fear are a part of life. And then, sometimes, there are souls born who come to the Earth to help the people remember the truth. Your child is such a one."

I paused a moment and let the words stand between us, giving her time to take in what I had said.

After a moment, I continued: "Your child will be a girl. She will remember what the people have forgotten and will teach them. She brings hope and will speak to them of the truth and the oneness which they seek. She will remember that she is one with the Gods and will act as such, healing and standing as a guide to the people on their inner journey. She will help the people remember that they are divine, that they are light, and that they come from the truth and will return to the truth."

I stopped my speaking and rose to add wood to the fire. Then I moved the water to the heat and began preparing some steepened brew. I did so to give her time, for the tears were standing as droplets unshed in her eyes, and her memory was stirring, but not yet ripe.

"Why do you tell me this?" she asked.

"I tell you this because of the child," I answered.

"As she is born, it is important that she remain at one with the Hierarchy and the Earth at the same time. This will help her remember."

I paused and then continued. "During her first years it will be necessary to teach her and to remind her so that she knows her calling and remembers who she is and what she has come to do."

She waited, as if weighing her words before she spoke. "I am seasoned, as you know," she said. "I have wondered for these months of my confinement why, now, I would conceive to bear a child. My husband and I, for many years, have had no life between us, and now …"

She paused, looking away from my eyes, and then, after a while, meeting them again. "Is it so?" she asked.

I heard the unspoken questions between us. She wanted to know if her destiny was tied to the unborn child and if bearing her would help to bring a change in the ways of the world.

She asked me if the child was her contribution to the unity of which I had just spoken and if she could find this unity through the passage of her calling into motherhood. She asked the question each mother asks silently before that moment of birthing. "Can what I now create bring the love and unity I have sought but been unable to find? Can I love this child enough to change the patterns of what is and create here what I know can be?"

She asked me if the world could change and if there could be love and if there could be acceptance, and peace, and the remembering.

As I heard her questions, I knew I had asked them also, as does each woman at the moment of procreation, and I answered her very softly, "Yes."

We looked at each other then in complete understanding, and I said, "It is time to begin."

She nodded and moved slowly and deftly to the stove where she finished preparing a brew of strong herbs and leaves to see us through the long night to come.

I watched her as she made me a small meal of bread and

figs and meat. As she moved, I saw that she was more assured, the fear gone—a new determination showing in the carriage of her body and within her womanness.

It stirred me deeply, for it affirmed my calling, and I was well rewarded. I let her prepare the food even though she was beginning her rhythm and the cycle of birth was upon her. This was the only way she could repay me, and it was a point of honor between us.

She gave to me the food, and I ate what she had prepared.

She nodded to me then and said, "I am now ready."

I began to speak. "The child is now moving into the tunnel. The vibrations of density from the Earth are now affecting her memory, and she is seeing only the light, forgetting the calling, and where she is, and why she is moving through the dimensions."

I paused and drank some brew and felt the knowing come into the mother, and then I continued. "The pattern of destiny is encoded into the soul, but for the child to remember it, she must be connected again to the memory as she is born. I can do this for a time, but it is your calling to instill the knowledge of divinity and the memory of her origin into the consciousness of your own child.

"When the child's soul is honored and upheld from the time of birth, there is much joy, for there is no experience of separation from the knowledge and the unity within. "The child is happy, well contented, fulfilled within, needing nothing in the way of the human to give her dignity or self-worthiness.

"The child creates from the inner potential and remembers her design. When this memory is real to the child, she has a sense of belonging and knows the angels as well as her physical playmates. The world is a beautiful place of discovery and creation. This is the way of the calling."

"How can I do this for my child?" she asked.

"Close your eyes and place your thoughts in the Seed of Light in the center of your body, in the place where your ribs come together in a point. There, yes, right below the heart. Breathe there, and you will feel your knowing. Ask that your light and the light of your child now be one. Imagine a light in the place where you hold the child in the womb. Now, as you feel and remember unity, expand your thinking to be a part of the light which your child brings. Feel your lights as one. Yes. Now as the rhythms and cycles of the child are felt in your body, you will feel the quickening more strongly, and the time between cycles will be shorter. Stay at one with the soul of the child now, and the birth will be easy and quick and clear."

We moved to the place which had been prepared for the birthing, and I continued to instruct her in the breathing and the merging. I told her I was also bonding with the child, and we continued for some time, feeling the soul of the child approaching now, more completely.

I instructed her to breathe into the light of the union between her and the child and to form a bridge of this light between her womb and the outside world. This would lead the child through the canal and into the world in light.

I asked her to keep the image of light inside and outside of her body at the same time, so that the child would see no separation and would be born in unity, remembering that the universe is a safe place to be.

Just before she was born, I sent out the call to the child and anchored universal light in her consciousness helping the mother to bridge the span between dimensions.

I showed the child the light of her calling and led her out of the womb into the density of Earth affirming her divinity:

"You are spirit, and so you shall remain,"
I said over and over again.

"Your truth shall be honored here.
You are free to create from the design within and live your potential and hold to the memory of your knowing."

When the mother had fulfilled the birthing, and the cleaning and ordering had been accomplished, we sat, the three, and bonded the light between us once again.

I instructed her, and she began the ritual of the birthing of light into form. She began connecting her seed with her child's seed again, feeling the bond between them.

She then brought light into the top of the child's head and drew it through the small body, creating a waterfall with the light. She did this several times until she felt the light steady and constant throughout her child's body. She then took the child's small feet in her hands and held the bottoms saying slowly and distinctly:

"You have chosen to come into form.
You have chosen to come into form.
You have chosen to come into form.
I anchor you into the mother Earth.
I anchor you into the mother Earth.
You have chosen this form.

You are light.
You are light.
You are light.

You are light and light you shall remain.
You are light and light you shall remain.
You are light and light you shall remain."

She said the words of the affirmation to her child with

intent. She placed one hand on her heart and the other on her baby's heart, speaking in the child's ear and saying:

"The bond that we have is through love;
what I teach you I teach from love;

what is not of your truth,
I give you permission to release.

I acknowledge your divinity and your spirit.

You have arrived on the planet Earth,
and you are a part of our family.

Know that you are creative and can achieve and
accomplish anything that you desire and that there are
no conditions on my love for you.

I will love you, always, without question."

As she finished the ritual of the birthing, she drew the child to her breast and they continued the joining.

Since she was more open in the first forty-eight hours after her birthing than at any other time in her life, I told her it was important to run the light of spirit through her body before she held the infant so that she would be filled with light when she held her. I also spoke of the need for her to be with her own spirit, while cherishing the bond with her child.

I instructed the mother to spend some moments each day joining with her child's Seed of Light and going with the child into the light of the Hierarchy and the place of truth. Since the first twenty-four months establishes the foundation between the hemispheres of consciousness, I told her that every day for two years the child would need to hear an affirmation that she is light.

I stayed with them for six months following the birthing. Each day I instructed the mother and sent the child a validation of her purpose and spoke to her the affirmation of light.

I grew to love the girl child and her mother, and we spent many hours talking, sharing, and loving.

I told the mother of the future of the child and gave her the teachings of the soul to share with her when she was older:

To always uphold the creativity of the child and encourage her uniqueness, affirming her child's divinity daily. To listen every morning to her child's dreams and, at night before bed, to listen to the experiences the child had that day.

This would help to integrate the unconscious and conscious processes of the child every twenty-four hours.

To have the child express all of her feelings without

judging them and to give the child an example of this through her own honest expression of emotion. This would explain the ways of the world and the laws of man, telling her why things are as they are. This would give her the understanding necessary to live here and respect others. If the child respected the ways of others, then others would respect her ways.

I spoke to the mother about the Earth as a learning place and about the lessons the child's soul had come to learn. I told her to teach the child that the lessons did not have to be learned through pain because pain is man-made and is not created from the Gods.

I instructed her and the child in the ways of the heart:

> To love unconditionally,
> To ask for the memory of the design,
> To join daily with the Seed of Light of those you love,
> To spend some moments together dreaming and being.

I stayed because of my calling, yes, but also because it was a respite from the travel and the aloneness of my outer existence. I explored the hills and valleys there and took the child with me, explaining to her about the Earth and the elements and the force fields. We went into the wind and the rain and under the trees and the stars. We touched the living things of the Earth every day, and the child learned about life.

As I was preparing to leave, I told the child about the truth within her; telling her of why she had come and of why I must go. I spoke to her as if she were of my years, sometimes using my tongue and sometimes using my mind.

She would listen, now barely sitting by herself, propped against the rocks beside her earthly home. She had clear almond eyes which reflected the memory of her inner truth and the knowledge within her soul. She was happy, smiling often, and content to be here.

When it was finished, we stood together in the door frame, the three as one—one in our calling, one in our being, one in our intention as women to create the wave of truth. I knew we had done well and I smiled, kissing them on each cheek.

I mounted Saschai then and rode forward, even now feeling the next calling. I was going in a direction which would bring me to Christ, for we had so appointed it. It would take many Earth years, and yet I did not sigh, for I was well contented. There was no place of lack within.

The child had filled me again with the presence of home, and it was fresh in my memory, as was the image of the prophecy and light the child had chosen to bring to Earth. As I rode away, the sun came over the mountain, and all the memories of all of the sun's risings came with it.

Resources

Beyond the Indigo Children: The New Children and the Coming of the Fifth World, P. M. H. Atwater, L.H.D.

Expecting Adam: A True Story of Birth, Rebirth, and Everyday Magic, Martha Beck. (Soul communications from unborn babies)

Return from Heaven: Beloved Relatives Reincarnated Within Your Family, Carol Bowman. (Studies of children who remember and information on pre-birth communication)

Cosmic Cradle: Souls Waiting in the Wings for Birth, Elizabeth M. Carman. (Study of pre-conception connections and memory of prelife)

The Mind of Your Newborn Baby, David B. Chamberlain. (Babies remember birth)

Diary of an Unborn Child: An Unborn Baby Speaks to Its Mother, Manuel D. Coudris. (Original perspective on soul experience in the womb)

Mother Link: Stories of Psychic Bonds Between Mother and Child, Cassandra Eason. (Readable, fun, and full of stories, both before and after birth)

Birthing the Babes of the Light: An Initiation to the Sacred Birth from the Brotherhoods and Sisterhoods of Light, Penelope A. Greenwell.

Stories of the Unborn Soul: The Mystery and Delight of Pre-Birth Communication, Elisabeth Hallett. (In-depth stories, including memories of pre-existence)

Soul Trek: Meeting Our Children on the Way to Birth, Elisabeth Hallett. (Information and stories)

Coming From the Light: Spiritual Accounts of Life Before Life, Sarah Hinze. (Inspiring stories and pre-birth communication)

Cheyenne: Journey to Birth, Mary G. McManus. (Record of prenatal conversation between mother and unborn child)

The Mother-to-Be's Dream Book: Understanding the Dreams of Pregnancy, Raïna M. Paris. (Poetic and practical book about communications)

The Call: Awakening The Angelic Human, Toni Elizabeth Sar'h Petrinovich.

Soleil Lithman: Integral Evolutionary Facilitator. Http://www.inlightenthebody.com/cellularconsciousness.htm.

Resources For
Welcoming Babies With Song

Omraam Mikhael Aivanhov. *Education Begins Before Birth*. Los Angeles: Prosveta USA, 1982. Can be ordered from Prosveta USA by calling 661-251-5412 or through the website http://www.prosveta-usa.com

Alfred A. Tomatis. *The Conscious Ear*. New York: Station Hill Press, 1991.

Mary Thienes Schunemann. *The Wonder of Lullabies*. Resource Songbook and CD to be ordered from www.naturallyyoucansing.com.

About The Author

**The soul is our greatest untapped resource.
Co-creating from the soul is the next
evolutionary step for our species.**
  - Flo Aeveia Magdalena

Flo Aeveia Magdalena is the founder of Soul Support Systems and the Heaven On Earth Global Community.

A respected visionary, futurist, author, channel, healer, teacher, and spiritual mid-wife, Flo Aeveia has worked throughout the world for 30 years with individuals and groups. She brings information, guidance and connection that catalyzes our potential and offers understanding of our personal life patterns.

Flo has developed programs that show us how to live from our greatest vibrational essence. We are then more congruent, and our interactions, choices and decisions are compatible with the pattern of our potential and links us to our part of the design. We can then show up in life, love more deeply and create from our inner resources and wisdom.

Flo published *I Remember Union: The Story Of Mary Magdalena*, a story of Magdalene and Christ that brings a message of hope about humanity's capacity to create a world of peace, honor, and union.

Her second book, *Sunlight On Water: A Manual For Soul-full Living* is a step–by-step guidebook that gives ways to connect with and access our evolving spirit.

About The Editor

Jayn Stewart and Flo Aeveia Magdalena have been collaborating on creative and educational projects for over twenty years. This is their third book.

As editor, Jayn assisted Flo in birthing the beautiful and inspiring story of Mary Magdalene, *I Remember Union.* She also edited *Sunlight on Water.*

Honoring Your Child's Spirit is especially dear to her heart because her daughters are now mothers, and she loves time spent with her young grandchildren.

This is her first book as an illustrator, but Jayn has been drawing all her life. As a child, her favorite subjects were horses, ballerinas, dogs, and rabbits. Now she is engaged in writing and illustrating books for children and adults. She finds her greatest inspirations in nature and the rich world of the imagination.